T0402860

TODAY'S SPORTS STARS

Cade Cunningham
Basketball Star

by Luke Hanlon

FOCUS READERS®
BEACON

www.focusreaders.com

Focus Readers is distributed by North Star Editions:
sales@northstareditions.com | 888-417-0195

Produced for Focus Readers by Red Line Editorial.

Photographs ©: Carlos Osorio/AP Images, cover, 1; Gregory Shamus/Getty Images Sport/Getty Images, 4, 20; Duane Burleson/AP Images, 6; Shutterstock Images, 8; Steven Ryan/Getty Images Sport/Getty Images, 11; Gregory Payan/AP Images, 13; Mitch Alcala/AP Images, 14; William Purnell/Icon Sportswire/AP Images, 17, 29; Charlie Riedel/AP Images, 18; Brian Fluharty/Getty Images Sport/Getty Images, 23; Nic Antaya/Getty Images Sport/Getty Images, 25; Red Line Editorial, 27

Library of Congress Cataloging-in-Publication Data
Library of Congress Cataloging-in-Publication Data is available on the Library of Congress website.

ISBN
979-8-88998-590-7 (hardcover)
979-8-88998-616-4 (paperback)
979-8-88998-607-2 (ebook pdf)
979-8-88998-599-0 (hosted ebook)

Printed in the United States of America
Mankato, MN
082025

About the Author

Luke Hanlon is a sportswriter and editor based in Minneapolis. He's written dozens of nonfiction sports books for kids and spends a lot of his free time watching his favorite Minnesota sports teams.

Table of Contents

CHAPTER 1

Clutch Cade

Cade Cunningham grabbed a rebound. The Detroit Pistons star dribbled up the court. Then he fired a pass. His teammate drained a three-pointer.

 **Cade Cunningham plays point guard. Point guards often run a team's offense.**

The Pistons were battling

the Miami Heat in overtime.

Cunningham recorded an **assist**

on his teammate's bucket. It was

Cunningham's 18th assist of the

game. That was a career high. And the basket put the Pistons up by one point.

Seconds later, Miami scored. The Heat took back the lead. But Cunningham responded. He scored a quick layup. The Pistons held on for a 125–124 win.

Did You Know?

Cunningham recorded a **triple-double** in the Pistons' win. He finished with 20 points, 18 assists, and 11 rebounds.

CHAPTER 2

Top Talent

Cade Cunningham was born on September 25, 2001. He grew up in Arlington, Texas. Cade's family was full of athletes. His father had played college football. And his brother played college basketball.

Arlington is about 20 miles (32 km) west of Dallas, Texas (pictured).

Cade played basketball and football in middle school. But he stopped playing football in high school. Instead, he put all his focus on basketball. He wanted to be like his brother.

Cade began at Bowie High School in 2016. The team's coach usually

Did You Know?

Cade played quarterback in middle school. The position helped him with his **vision**. That made him a better point guard.

didn't let freshmen play much. But Cade was different. He started right away.

Cade changed schools after his second year. He wanted to prepare for college basketball. So, he switched to Montverde Academy.

That school was in Florida. Cade played with other top **prospects** there. And the team faced some of the best players in the country.

Cade thrived at his new school. He improved his jump shot. He also impressed **scouts** with his defense. In 2019, Cade entered his senior year. Montverde didn't lose a single game. The Eagles finished the season 25–0.

Scouts thought Cade was one of the best high school players in the

Cade averaged 13.9 points, 6.4 assists, and 4.2 rebounds per game as a senior in high school.

nation. Many colleges wanted him to play for their school. Cade's older brother was an assistant coach at Oklahoma State University. So, Cade decided to go there. He started college in the fall of 2020.

CHAPTER 3

One and Done

Cade Cunningham was used to facing talented players. He had no problem with the jump to college. Cunningham tallied 21 points in his first game. He also grabbed 10 rebounds.

 **Cade Cunningham led Oklahoma State to six straight wins to start the 2020–21 season.**

Great performances from the first-year star became common. In February 2021, Oklahoma State faced Oklahoma. Oklahoma was ranked No. 7 in the country. But Cunningham was ready. He faked out defenders at the rim. And he drained long three-point shots. Cunningham finished the game with 40 points. The Oklahoma State Cowboys won 94–90.

Cunningham continued his terrific play in the Big 12 **tournament**.

 Oklahoma State was ranked No. 11 in the nation before the 2021 NCAA tournament.

The Cowboys faced Baylor in the semifinals. Baylor had lost only one game all season. But Cunningham couldn't be stopped. He hit tough shots over defenders. And he set up teammates with great passes.

Cunningham dished out five assists in the semifinals of the Big 12 tournament.

Oklahoma State beat Baylor 83–74. Next, Cunningham scored 29 points in the championship game. But the Cowboys lost to Texas.

Oklahoma State had an early exit in the NCAA tournament. The team lost in the second round. Cunningham was ready to move on. He entered the National Basketball Association (NBA) **Draft**. The Detroit Pistons had the No. 1 pick. They chose Cunningham.

Did You Know?

In 2021, Cunningham won awards for being the best freshman and best player in the Big 12. He was only the fourth player to win both in the same season.

CHAPTER 4

Going Pro

Moving to the NBA was a big step. Cunningham scored only two points in his first game. But he adjusted quickly. Soon, he recorded his first NBA triple-double.

 **Cunningham averaged 17.4 points per game in his first NBA season.**

Cunningham kept up the great play all year. He had 25 games with 20 points or more. After the season, he made the NBA All-**Rookie** Team.

The next year, Cunningham injured his leg. His season ended after just 12 games. By 2023–24,

Did You Know?

In 2023, Cunningham donated a total of $70,000 to several schools. The money helped provide snacks and supplies to students.

 In 2023–24, Cunningham recorded 22.7 points and 7.5 assists per game.

he was back on the court.

The Pistons struggled to win games, though. They finished with the league's worst record.

Detroit hired a new coach before the 2024–25 season. The team also signed some **veterans**. The Pistons' younger players continued to improve, too.

Having better teammates helped Cunningham. Defenders couldn't focus on him as much. He got more chances to score and to show off his passing skills. In November, he recorded four triple-doubles.

Cunningham made his first All-Star team in 2025. His strong

Cunningham racked up his eighth triple-double of the season in a February 2025 win over the Charlotte Hornets.

play lifted the Pistons to their best season since 2015–16. The team even made the playoffs. The future looked bright for Detroit's young star.

Cade Cunningham

- Height: 6 feet, 6 inches (198 cm)
- Weight: 220 pounds (100 kg)
- Birth date: September 25, 2001
- Birthplace: Arlington, Texas
- High school: Bowie High School (Arlington, Texas); Montverde Academy (Montverde, Florida)
- College team: Oklahoma State University (Stillwater, Oklahoma) (2020–21)
- NBA team: Detroit Pistons (2021–)
- Major awards: Big 12 Player of the Year (2021); NBA All-Rookie Team (2022); NBA All-Star (2025)

Detroit

Stillwater

Arlington

Montverde

Focus Questions

Write your answers on a separate piece of paper.

1. Write a paragraph that explains the main ideas of Chapter 4.

2. What do you think is Cade Cunningham's most useful skill? Why?

3. Which team did Oklahoma State defeat in the semifinals of the 2021 Big 12 tournament?
   - **A.** Oklahoma
   - **B.** Baylor
   - **C.** Texas

4. How did playing quarterback help Cunningham become a better point guard?
   - **A.** It helped him become a better defender.
   - **B.** It helped him become a better shooter.
   - **C.** It helped him keep track of teammates and make good passes.

5. What does **thrived** mean in this book?

*Cade **thrived** at his new school. He improved his jump shot. He also impressed scouts with his defense.*

    A. grew and succeeded

    B. struggled and lost

    C. avoided playing

6. What does **adjusted** mean in this book?

*Moving to the NBA was a big step. Cunningham scored only two points in his first game. But he **adjusted** quickly. Soon, he recorded his first NBA triple-double.*

    A. became confused

    B. stayed the exact same

    C. got used to something

Answer key on page 32.

Glossary

assist
A pass that leads directly to a teammate scoring.

draft
A system that allows teams to acquire new players coming into a league.

prospects
Players who are likely to be successful in the future.

rookie
A professional athlete in his or her first year.

scouts
People whose jobs involve looking for talented young players.

tournament
A competition that includes many teams.

triple-double
A game in which a player has double-digit numbers in three categories. The categories are often points, assists, and rebounds.

veterans
Players who have been in a league for a long time.

vision
The ability to see what is happening during a game and to understand where other players will be as a play develops.

To Learn More

BOOKS

Giedd, Steph. *Detroit Pistons*. Press Box Books, 2024.

Kjartansson, Kjartan Atli. *Legends of the NBA*. Abbeville Press, 2022.

Whiting, Jim. *The Story of the Detroit Pistons*. Creative Education, 2023.

NOTE TO EDUCATORS

Visit **www.focusreaders.com** to find lesson plans, activities, links, and other resources related to this title.

Index

A
All-Star team, 24
Arlington, Texas, 9

B
Baylor, 17–18
Big 12 tournament,
16–18
Bowie High School,
10–11

D
Detroit Pistons, 5–7, 19,
23–25

F
Florida, 12

M
Miami Heat, 6–7
Montverde Academy,
11–12

N
NBA All-Rookie Team, 22
NCAA tournament, 18

O
Oklahoma State
University, 13, 16–18

P
playoffs, 25

T
Texas, 18